Ra Press
100 Kennedy Drive #53
South Burlington, VT 05403

cover photograph: MEN ON CURE CHAIRS ON CURE

PORCH courtesy of HISTORIC SARANAC LAKE

ISBN 978-1-387-88563-3

CURE COTTAGE & OTHER PLAYS

Charles Watts

Contents

Cure Cottage

Characters

Robert Louis Stevenson (*novelist and poet*)

Adelaide Crapsey (*poet*)

Christy Mathewson (*baseball player*)

NOTE: All three characters listed above are wearing pajamas and spend most of their time tucked tightly into "cure couch" lounge chairs wrapped in thick woolen blankets.

Dr. Becuum (*a woman of indeterminate age*)

Disclaimer: Some of the dialogs of the three main characters are taken from their writings or utterances.

NOTE: Actors should feel free to cough whenever sputum or dialog makes it seem proper.

The porch of a cure cottage in Saranac Lake, NY on a sunny and frigid mid-winter day in the mountains. There are three "cure chairs" or "cure recliners," each of which has a small table beside it. There is a large thermometer on the wall; it reads -10. Adelaide Crapsey is sitting up in the middle recliner, covered in heavy blankets. She is scribbling in a notebook. She stops and reads.

Adelaide: Still as
On windless nights
The moon-cast shadows are,
So still will be my heart when I
Am dead.

Dr. Becuum: (*from offstage*) Adelaide! Are you writing again?

Adelaide: No, Dr. Becuum. Just testing the remains of my voice.

(*Dr. Becuum enters, helping a large man in pajamas walk. Adelaide quickly stuffs her notebook under her blanket and smiles innocently.*)

Dr. Becuum: This just won't do, Adelaide. You must restrict your writing to a maximum of half an hour a day. You are here to be cured. Rest, relax, breath the cold mountain air. That writing will be the death of you. Speaking of which, that was a pretty depressing lyric. Try to think positively.

(*Dr. Becuum helps the man into bed and tucks him in with the blankets.*)

Adelaide: I know, I know. But what am I to do? How can I bear lying here all day with nothing to do but freeze my lungs? Coming here was all a horrible mistake.

Dr. Becuum: There are no mistakes, my dear. It is the perfect temperature for your cure. (*She goes to the thermometer and looks at it*) Minus 10...ideal! Look here, I've brought you some company. Adelaide, this is Christy.

(*Adelaide reaches over and extends her hand. Christy tries to clasp it, and both break out in a fit of coughing.*)

Adelaide: (*regaining her wind*) Charmed, I'm sure.

Christy: 'Tis a pleasure to meet you.

Dr. Becuum: Get to know each other. It will give you something to do. Try not to talk too much. It could try the strength of your lungs. Tuberculosis is not a disease for the weak-willed. Control yourselves, speak softly, use short sentences. This is the path to recovery.

(*Dr. Becuum exits.*)

Adelaide: Christy, eh? Short for Christopher?

Christy: Exactly. Precisely. On target.

Adelaide: How long have you suffered?

Christy: Seven long years. An early version of hell, I fear.

Adelaide: Seven years! Is that some kind of record?

Christy: (*laughing and coughing*) I have many records, but I hope this is not the one I'm remembered for.

Adelaide: My word...a man of many records. What is it you do?

Christy: Nowadays I do nothing but cough and spit. But back in the day, I was a pitcher.

Adelaide: You were the bearer of water?

Christy: No, no. A baseball pitcher.

Adelaide: How wonderful. An athlete. I have never met one.

Christy: You still have not. I was once, but am no more.

Adelaide: When you were once an athlete, were you famous? Would I know your name?

Christy: Christy Mathewson.

Adelaide: No! Really? The Christy Mathewson?

Christy: The very same.

Adelaide: Why, I read about you all the time, even though I am not a true sports fan. No one who peruses the news could not know you. Just this year, as I recall, you won 25 games and pitched in the World Series.

Christy: I fear you are mistaken. That was back in 1913. I haven't pitched since 1916.

Adelaide: The tuberculosis must have gone to your brain, sir. It is 1913.

Christy: I beg your pardon? It is 1925.

Adelaide: Poor man. I didn't realize this kind of fantasy was a consequence of our disease.

Christy: Nor did I. But you are the one that is suffering from fantasy.

Adelaide: No, no. This is not good. Let us forget about time and get to know each other. Did you come down with tuberculosis while you were pitching?

Christy: Not really. I was serving in France during the Great War and was exposed to Mustard Gas while at a training exercise.

Adelaide: War? What war?

Christy: The Great one.

Adelaide: Sir, I believe you are addled. I know of no such war.

Christy: Then you know nothing of the world.

Adelaide: I am quite well educated, thank you. Great War indeed. So let's see: mustard gas, great war...when did the tuberculosis attack?

Christy: Soon after the mustard gas. Weak lungs. I'm not used to weakness.

Adelaide: I, unfortunately, am. I have always been weak of body.

Christy: What is it that you do, Adelaide?

Adelaide: I am a poet.

Christy: A poet? I didn't realize people could get paid for that.

Adelaide: We don't. We do it for love.

Christy: I guess we are alike in that. I pitched for love of the game.

(*Dr. Becuum enters, assisting another man.*)

Dr. Becuum: Chatter, chatter, chatter. I see you two are getting along.

Christy: Adelaide is a charming woman, if a bit confused by the date.

Adelaide: And Christy is a charming man, if a bit confused by the date.

Dr. Becuum: Let us not worry about time. We have an eternity to think about that. (*She tucks the new man into his cure couch*) Adelaide, Christy, this is Robert.

(*Adelaide reaches over and extends her hand. Robert tries to clasp it, and both break out in a fit of coughing.*)

Adelaide: (*regaining her wind*) Robert, welcome to your new home. I hope you do not come from somewhere in the south. Here on our porch it is as cold as the Arctic.

Robert: Pleased to meet you, Adelaide. I am from Edinburgh and accustomed to a winter's chill.

Christy: (*Waving across the beds*) And I from Pennsylvania, also home to dreary winters.

Adelaide: Christy and I have just begun to acquaint ourselves. He is a baseball player and I...

13

Christy: She is a poet, or so she says. I am...was...a pitcher. A pitcher is not a player, just a thrower of balls.

Robert: I have heard of the game. An inferior form of cricket, as I recall.

Christy: Inferior! Baseball is an art!

Robert: Art is painting, poetry, theater. Baseball is a game for children and those who do not grow up.

Christy: Balderdash! How superficial! Adelaide, do you follow the theater?

Adelaide: I do. My poetry is a form of theater, only with just one actor.

Christy: And you, Robert, are you familiar with the theatrical arts?

Robert: I am.

Christy: Consider this. If you've ever been around a group of actors, you've noticed, no doubt, that they can talk of nothing else under the sun but acting. It's exactly the same with baseball players. Your heart must be in your work. If it is, your life becomes a work of art.

Robert: Well said, young man. I apologize for my rude remark. Are you a writer as well as a baseball player?

Christy: Apology accepted. I am not a writer, but I do have an education and a mind. Every man has a sane spot somewhere.

Robert: I like that. Can I borrow it?

Christy: For what?

Robert: I, like Adelaide, am a writer. I am always looking for a good line. Adelaide, I worry we are ignoring you. I have a question. Christy said you are a poet. Should I know of your work?

Adelaide: I fear not. I have never had the honor of being published. It is, however, my hope that that shall change soon. While here, in this frozen hell, I have developed a new form of poetry, uniquely American. I hope to change the face of verse.

Robert: Such ambition! In a way, I agree with you. There is no progress whatever. Everything is just the same as it was thousands, and tens of thousands, of years ago. The outward form changes. The essence does not change.

Adelaide: I must disagree. Outward form is not just rhetoric, it can be meaning in and of itself. The way something is said can be as important as what is said.

Christy: What nonsense. Form and substance are just words. Reality is what God gives us. All of this is just idle chatter.

Robert: To be idle requires a strong sense of personal identity. If God has given me this body and this disease, I reject him.

Christy: Heretic! God is the only true reality, the only true beauty. Only a dog would reject his majesty.

Robert: You think dogs will not be in heaven? I tell you, they will be there long before any of us.

Adelaide: Listen to yourselves! Neither of you has any clue about what heresy is. My own father was accused and convicted of heresy, and he was the holiest man I have ever known.

Christy: Only God and his Son are holy. And the written word, the bible, the literal truth of the world.

Adelaide: The bible is a metaphor for how we should behave. No one literally rises from the dead or cures the leper with just his words. That, in fact, was exactly my father's so-called heresy.

Christy: If you believe that, then you, too, are a heretic.

Robert: You are both wrong. Heaven is not the goal and words are not the path. To be what we are, and to become what we are capable of becoming, is the only end of life.

(*Dr. Becuum enters with a tray of glasses filled with milk. She places one on each table beside the patients.*)

Dr. Becuum: Here is your afternoon milk. Drink up, now. I can hear you from the other room and you are wearing out your lungs with abstract and absurd discussions. Why not quiet down and read a book? It will do you good to rest.

Robert: Books are good enough in their own way, but they are a poor substitute for life.

Dr. Becuum: Well, if you want a long life, you must rest. Dinner will be served soon, and you want to have the strength to eat heartily.

Robert: There is only one difference between a long life and dinner: that in the dinner, the sweets come last.

Dr. Becuum: So negative, Robert.

Robert: Realistic, I call it.

Dr. Becuum: Don't take yourself so seriously. Forget yourself and enjoy the journey.

Robert: To forget oneself is to be happy. I shall attempt to follow your advice.

Dr. Becuum: Excellent. Now drink up.

(*The patients chug their milk, cough, and put the glasses down. Dr. Becuum collects them on her tray.*)

Dr. Becuum: Well done.

(*She exits.*)

Christy: What an arrogant woman. Thinks she know everything. I am beginning to loathe her.

Robert: I regard her with an indifference closely bordering on aversion.

Adelaide: So cynical! You say you are a writer...is your writing all so depressing?

Robert: Most of my writing is a total fraud. Adventure stories and tales of the supernatural. A book of children's poems. Nothing of substance. Some were popular, but none great.

Adelaide: At least you have published. That is something. What are some of your titles? Perhaps I have read them.

Robert: Treasure Island was my first so-called success.

Christy: Treasure Island! No! I read that as a child. What a tale!

Robert: Neo-romantic nonsense.

Adelaide: I fear you are pulling our collective legs, Robert. Treasure Island was written years ago by Robert Louis Stevenson. He has been dead for almost two decades.

Robert: Old and young, we are all on our last cruise. I am, however, very much alive.

Adelaide: Are you mental? It's 1913 and Robert Louis Stevenson is dead!

Christy: Are you mental? It's 1925!

Robert: Are you mental? It's 1887!

(*Dr. Becuum enters. She is carrying a clipboard.*)

Dr. Becuum: What a commotion!

Christy, Adelaide, and Robert (*together*): What the hell is going on here?

Dr. Becuum: No, not hell. More like a waiting room.

Adelaide: More like a loony bin. Why did you put me here with these two creatures?

Christy: My exact question.

Robert: I guess that makes it unanimous.

Dr. Becuum: Far from an asylum. You are here because, well, all of you were in cure cottages at some time. Your experiences were similar, so we thought you would feel more comfortable in an environment you were familiar with.

Adelaide: How can I trust someone who ends a sentence with a preposition?

Dr. Becuum: Both a teacher and a poet! You three have been such a pleasure to watch. But now it is time to get down to business.

Robert: How can we trust someone who starts a sentence with a coordinating conjunction?

Dr. Becuum: Robert! Such a card! You and Adelaide are so much alike.

Robert: I am published. She is not.

Dr. Becuum: But she will be. After she passed, her work was recognized, and she is now considered the mother of the Cinquain, a five-line form similar to the Haiku.

Adelaide: Passed? I'm passed.

Dr. Becuum: Yes, my dear. All of you passed some time ago.

Christy: Say it ain't so!

Dr. Becuum: It is so.

Christy, Adelaide, and Robert (*together*): What the hell is going on here?

Dr. Becuum: I told you. This is a waiting room for your next life, a place where you contemplate what is important, what you need to work on to become truly happy and enlightened. I think it has gone well.

Christy: All I've learned is that these supposed intellectuals are a bunch of heretics with no relationship to the true God.

Dr. Becuum: And that is why you will be reborn to a farm family as an awkward girl. They will be secure in their faith. You will be the first of your clan to go to college and will question that faith. What you decide will determine your future lives. (*She goes to Christy and puts her hand over his eyes. He slumps into sleep. She glances back and forth between Robert and Adelaide.*) He will be sleeping for many years, but it will be peaceful.

Robert: And what of me?

Dr. Becuum: A strong and willful farm wife. You will learn what it means to be unknown and loved.

(*She goes to Robert and puts a hand over his eyes. He descends into sleep.*)

Adelaide: What a waste. He is...was...such a great writer.

Dr. Becuum: He learned what he needed to learn. Now he will learn something new.

Adelaide: And what of me?

Dr. Becuum: You will be a farmer, a devout believer in the almighty and a lover of nature. You will marry, well, Robert, in his new incarnation. You will have a daughter who questions everything. You will pray for her soul when she rejects all that you believe. If you are lucky, you will suffer and find peace.

Adelaide: You mean Christy? Christy will be our child?

Dr. Becuum: Of course! That's why we brought you all here together. You won't remember anything, of course, but your souls will be connected.

Adelaide: I don't understand.

Dr. Becuum: Understanding is vastly overrated. Could you do me a favor?

Adelaide: Whatever you say.

Dr. Becuum: Read me your favorite poem. One of your own, please.

Adelaide: (*She takes out her notebook, looks through it, and reads*)

> Just now,
> Out of the strange
> Still dusk...as strange, as still...
> A white moth flew...Why am I grown
> So cold?

Dr. Becuum: Very fitting. I love that one, too. Would you like me to recite my favorite?

Adelaide: You know my work?

Dr. Becuum: Indeed I do.

> Wouldst thou find my ashes? Look
> In the pages of my book;
> And as these pages thy hand doth turn,
> Know here is my funeral urn.

(*Dr. Becuum goes to Adelaide and puts her hand over her eyes. She sleeps.*)

Dr. Becuum: (*cont*) Sleep now, my child. The best, God willing and the creeks don't rise, is yet to come.

Darkness.

The End

The Current Below

A Play in One Act

<u>Cast of Characters</u>

Lila: In her mid-80's, but in good health.

John: In his late-80's, suffering from dementia.

Charlie: Their grandson.

INT. CABIN EARLY EVENING

A rustic cabin. There is a double bed, a kitchen table, sink, shelves for plates and books, cabinets for kitchen equipment, a refrigerator, a wood burning stove. John is at the table, writing in a notebook. Lila is at the sink, washing dishes. John writes, scratches out, rewrites.

John: Through. Chew. Blue. Grew...True!

(*He writes furiously.*)

John: Night. Trite. Flight...Light!

(*He writes furiously.*)

John: Night. Light. Bite. Kite. White...Plight!

(*He writes furiously.*)

(*Lila dries her hands and goes over John and stands behind him, putting her hands on his shoulders. He stands up suddenly, knocking her to the floor.*)

John: Don't touch me! Who are you? I got a gun!

Lila: It's me, John. Just me.

John: Me? I don't know a me. Who...oh...Lila. Are you alright?

Lila: I'll be fine. I just wanted to see what you're working on.

John: A new poem. One finally came into my head.

Lila: Why that's wonderful! Can you read it to me?

John: It's not done yet...just a start.

Lila: Go ahead. I'd like to hear it.

John: Very well.

(*He stands and reads from the notebook.*)

An hour more than halfway through
The flaming forge of night
The village smithy out of true
Doth grapple with the light
His large and sinewy hands enfold
The blackness of his plight

Lila: Oh dear...

John: What do you think? Do you like it?

Lila: Well...oh dear...it's a bit derivative.

John: Derivative? I never write derivative! Everything comes from the pitiful remains of my mind!

Lila: Um, I seem to recall a poem by Henry Wadsworth Longfellow. The Village Blacksmith.

John: Longfellow? That old fart? Why would I steal from him?

(*Lila goes to the bookshelf and takes out a volume, opens it and reads.*)

Lila: Under a spreading chestnut-tree
The village smithy stands;
The smith, a mighty man is he,
With large and sinewy hands;

And then later:

They love to see the flaming forge

John: Dammit! That man's a thief! How did he get my poem?

Lila: Honey, he died in 1882. You just wrote yours today.

John: Today? Why, this is the best work I've done in...today?

Lila: Yes, dear.

John: Christ on a crutch. It's getting worse, isn't it?

Lila: You have good days and bad days. It's ok, John. There are some good lines that are all your own. You even threw in some rhymes, which is quite different for you. Almost innovative.

John: Bullshit. It's just another goddamn regression. That's how I wrote when I was six. Fuck this alpsenheimer!

Lila: Alzheimer's. Good days and bad days. Today is good. You wrote a poem.

John: I wrote drivel. Drool. Dogshit.

(*He picks up the notebook and spits on it, then slumps into the chair, face in his hands.*)

(*Lila moves to massage his shoulders. He spins and pushes her back.*)

John: (*cont*) Leave me alone. Who the hell are you?

Lila: It's me, John. Lila.

John: Lila. That's my wife. Where is she?

Lila: She'll be back soon.

(*She goes back to the sink and continues doing dishes. There is a knock on the door. John leaps up and grabs a pistol from a drawer, points it at the door.*)

John: Go away! There's nobody here!

Charlie: (*off stage*) It's me, grampa. Charlie. Can I come in?

Lila takes the gun from John and puts it back in the drawer.

Lila: It's just Charlie. Come on in, honey!

(*Charlie enters. He goes to hug Lila.*)

Charlie: Hey there, grammy!

(*John goes to the drawer, takes out the pistol, and points it at Charlie.*)

John: Leave her alone, you bastard!

Lila: Put that down, John! It's your grandson Charlie.

John: Hell it is. Charlie's like this high.

(*He holds his free hand about waist high. Charlie moves toward him.*)

Charlie: Hey, grampa. It's me!

(*John points the gun at Charlie and pulls the trigger.*)

(*There is a click. He looks at the gun, confused. Charlie takes it from him.*)

Lila: Shame on you, John.

(*She takes the gun from Charlie and puts it back in the drawer.*)

Lila: (*cont*) That's why I hide the bullets. He tried to shoot me three times this week.

John: He...who...why...

Lila: Give your gramps a hug, Charlie. He gets like this sometimes.

(*Charlie tries to hug John, who pulls away.*)

John: Keep your hands off me!

Charlie: OK, OK, grampa. Let's just sit down for a minute.

John: Charlie's six. You can't fool me.

Charlie: I grew up, gramps. You'll remember in a bit.

(*They all sit down at the table.*)

John: I remember, I remember. You were here yesterday. We went fishing in the pond and caught a bluegill. You were so excited, but afraid to touch it.

Charlie: Hey, you're right! I was six when we did that. It was a great day.

John: It...it was...a great day. What's today?

Charlie: Friday.

John: Friday. Don't we do something on Friday? Did I miss work?

Lila: You're retired, honey. You just need to rest up and relax.

John: Relax? I've got papers to grade!

Lila: No more grading. You left the University ten years ago.

John: But my students...

Lila: They still remember you. That young poet you liked so much. Jim Lundy, sent a note last week.

John: Jim? Yes, he has talent. (to Charlie) Are you Jim?

Charlie: No, grampa. Maybe he'll come by soon.

John: Good. That would be nice.

Lila: Are you OK now?

John: I'm always OK now. It's the past and future I have trouble with. It's always now for me.

Charlie: That's my grampa! Welcome back.

John: Back? Where did I go?

Lila: Just a little trip down memory lane.

John: Hey...Charlie...good to see you, boy.

Charlie: Always good to see you, gramps.

John: Say, I'm a little tired. I think I'll go down to the pond and try to catch something for dinner.

Charlie: Great idea. Can I join you?

John: Thanks, but no. I need to be alone for awhile. Think things through.

(*John gets up and heads for the door.*)

John: (*cont*) See you in a while.

(*He exits. Lila puts her hands to her face and begins to cry.*)

Lila: I can't take it anymore...

(*Charlie gets up and rubs her shoulders.*)

Charlie: It'll be alright, gramma. It'll be alright.

Lila: No, it won't! He's turning into a monster!

Charlie: You've been able to handle it so far.

Lila: I've handled nothing. I've been nothing. All my life I've been just the wife of the great poet, the wife of the great professor. I'm old now, and I've never done a damn thing for myself, never been anything myself. A total waste of my life.

Charlie: But...but...

Lila: No buts about it, Charlie. I just want to get this all over with. I give up. I want out.

Charlie: Maybe it's time to get professional help. There's that dementia facility in town.

Lila: He'll never agree to that. We talked about it before, even went for a visit. He saw all those people wandering around, looking for a door, any exit, drooling and frightened and totally out of it. Said he'd rather shoot himself first.

Charlie: He'd get used to it. Or forget about it. Half the time he doesn't know where he is or who we are. At least they know how to deal with folks in his condition.

Lila: I know that, honey, but how can I do that to him? I might as well just accept what he is, what he's becoming, and forget about myself. Wouldn't that be the humane thing to do?

Charlie: I think the humane thing to do is get him into a place where he can live out the rest of his life without being a burden on others. Isn't that what he would want if he was thinking clearly?

Lila: Funny. He used to tell me to tie him on the back of a donkey and send him out into the desert if he ever lost his mind.

Charlie: Perhaps the facility is his donkey and his desert. Perhaps this is what he would want.

(*There is a cry from offstage.*)

John: Help! Help!

(*Charlie runs out the door. Lila stands in the opening and watches.*)

Charlie: (*offstage*) Hang on, grampa!

John: (*offstage*) Go away! Help! Go away!

Charlie: (*offstage*) I've got you, grampa!

John: (*offstage*) Leave me alone! You got to let me do it!

Charlie: (*offstage*) No...no...no...that's right, that's right...come with me.

(*Lila moves aside and Charlie and John enter. They are both soaking wet.*)

Lila: My god, my god...what happened?

John: He should of let me...let me

Charlie: He was in the pond. I think he was trying to drown himself.

(*Lila rushes to John and envelopes him.*)

Lila: John, John how could you...why...

(*John pulls away, shivering.*)

John: I was just....fishing.

Lila goes to a cabinet and pulls out some towels. She hands one to John.

Lila: Go dry off and change your clothes.

(John exits to the bedroom, head down. Lila hands a towel to Charlie, then goes to a closet and gets a shirt and pair of pants, hands them to Charlie.)

Lila: *(cont)* You can change in the bathroom.

(Charlie exits to the bathroom. John enters in dry clothes.)

Lila: *(cont)* Lie down on the couch, honey. You look like you could use a nap.

(John lays down on the couch. Lila covers him with a blanket. Charlie enters in dry clothes.)

Charlie: Sure feels better. Pretty cold in that pond.

(Lila goes to a coat rack and puts on her coat.)

Lila: I'm going into town to talk to the people at the facility.

Lila: *(cont)* Can you stay with John? I won't be long.

Charlie: No problem. I'll take good care of him.

(Lila exits. John twists and turns on the couch.)

Charlie: Grampa, do you want me to read you something?

John: Read? Yes, read. Something from one of my books.

Charlie: Good for you...the real John is back. How about one from "The Current Below?"

John: Read "The Blue Heron."

(*Charlie goes to the bookshelf and takes down a book, leafs through, finds the poem.*)

Charlie: Here you go:

A blue heron slides
Under the berm of the pond
Under the red tree semaphoring
Fall is upon us
A small fish vaults
Toward the leaves
Water bug in sight
Then on its lips
The same fish my grandson
Caught and released last summer
The heron launches its beak
Raises its head
Tries to swallow
But the insect shakes free
Rescuing despair
From the jaws of joy

John: Nice. Did you write that, Jim?

Charlie: Not Jim...Charlie. You wrote it, grampa.

John: Well, very good. I'm glad you became a writer.

(*John lays back on the couch and tries to sleep.*)

Charlie: I'm going to read on the porch for awhile.

(*There is no response from John. Charlie exits.*)

(*John sits up and looks around. He rises and begins opening drawers and closets, searching for something. He finds a box of bullets, takes the gun from the drawer and loads it. He goes to the table, opens his notebook and stares at it. He puts the gun to his head, then puts it down.*)

John: Green...bean...screen...scene...

He begins to write furiously. We hear a car pull up.

Charlie: (*offstage*) How'd it go, gramma?

Lila: (*offstage*) Good, if you call it that. They have a bed open.

(*Lila and Charlie enter. John leaps up with the gun in hand and points it at Charlie.*)

John: Stop right there!

Charlie: It's OK, grampa. Give me the gun.

(*John fires off three quick, loud shots. Lila screams. Charlie runs his hands down his shirt. No blood.*)

John: Stay back, stay back! I won't miss twice!

(*Lila goes toward John and tries to take the gun. He pulls back, points it at his temple and pulls the trigger. A shot rings out. John staggers but does not fall. Lila takes the gun, and John sits unsteadily on the couch.*)

Charlie: What...how...

Lila: Blanks. I could never kill anything. Just wanted to have something to keep the varmints away.

(*She goes to John and looks at his head.*)

Lila: (*cont*) Well, the wadding caused a bit of a bump, but otherwise no damage. Honey, why don't you get your coat. We're going to town. I want to introduce you to some new friends.

(*John puts on a coat and all three exit.*)

Curtain.

THE PURITY OF WATER

Character

Juliet: The Doyen of the cultural scene in a small but upscale town in the Adirondacks. She is in her 50's, is slender and fit, wears black, and has flaming red hair.

Albert: A retired Shakespearean actor in his 70's. Bald, out of shape, with a major league pot belly.

Silvia: An Italian actress, once married to a famous film director. In her 40's, she is both stylish and beautiful.

Edward: A young poet, in his 20's. He looks, well, poetic.

Duke: Juliet's camp caretaker, in his 40's. Strong and in the prime of life.

Set

The main room of a rustic but upscale cabin. The furniture is Adirondack style, made of birch branches and hardwood. There are four chairs, a dining room table with a candelabra in the center, a fireplace, and a multi-tiered shelf overstuffed with books. Near the fireplace is a plain wooden bench, large enough to hold two people. On the other side of the fireplace is a small serving table with cabinets underneath. A large carafe of wine, five wine glasses, an ice bucket, and a small vial of liquid are on it. On the dining room table is a manila folder stuffed with papers. There are entrances on both sides of the stage.

(*Juliet is at the serving table. She picks up the vial of liquid and pours it into the carafe of wine, stirs it, and puts the empty vial in the cabinet. We hear the sound of a motor. Juliet moves to center stage and looks out over the audience.*)

Juliet: Oh wonderful! They're here.

(*She goes to both tables and makes sure all is in its proper place. Albert and Duke enter. Albert takes off a parka and throws it on a chair.*)

Juliet: (*cont*) Albert! How fabulous to see you! (*She hugs him and kisses both cheeks.*)

Albert: I'm sure it is. I usually don't come to such rustic locations. Paris, London, Rome...those are my natural homes.

Juliet: Still full of yourself, I see.

Albert: The truth will out.

Juliet: (*Stepping back to look Albert over.*) You look...terrible, my dear. Have you been sick?

Albert: I have seen better days. Sometimes I indulge in too much of the good things life offers.

Juliet: Sex, drugs, rock and roll?

Albert: You know me too well.

(*Juliet turns to Duke.*)

Juliet: Duke, where are the others?

Duke: They hadn't shown up yet. Mr. Albert said I must bring him over right away, that he had not slept a wink, that it was deathly cold on the dock, and that, come what may, I must put him in the boat or he would vanish into thin air.

Juliet: Albert, you are so faint hearted. Duke, take the boat back to the dock immediately and pick up Silvia and Edward. It is vital that they be here tonight.

(*Duke turns without a word and exits.*)

Albert: Good riddance. How can you stand to have that yokel around you? The only thing he said on the way over was "cold enough for you?"

Juliet: Such pomposity! Duke is a fine and sincere helper. When I'm out here on the island, he is all I have to keep the place up. He can do carpentry, plumbing, electrical work, and is a strong as a young bull. Not bad looking either.

Albert: I see. You utilize his skills for more than just housework.

Juliet: Oh hush. You of all people should not judge others.

Albert: By that you mean?

Juliet: You were my first love. Your MacBeth in Central Park was superb. You stole my young heart, seduced me, took the flower of my virginity, and vanished into thin air.

Albert: Your mother should have taught you about the vagaries of artists. You wanted all I gave you. That should have been enough for any young acolyte.

Juliet: Worry not, dear Albert. I forgave you long ago. How long has it been?

Albert: 20, 30 years? A lifetime ago.

Juliet: It might seem so. For you I was just another stage-door girl. For me, it was first love, and my first lost love.

Albert: From what I read in the international press, I was not your last.

Juliet: Heavens no! One should not dwell in the past. Today is all that really matters. I do want to thank you for coming. I did not expect you to accept my invitation.

Albert: I'm between roles. Shylock last year, Prospero in January. (*He looks to the door, then tries to embrace Juliet.*) Since it appears we have a bit of time alone, should we relive old times?

(*Juliet pushes him away.*)

Juliet: Still on the prowl? I think not. Have you looked in the mirror lately?

(*She pats his gut.*)

Albert: A man is not a man without a shed over his tools.

Juliet: I suspect the tools are a bit rusty. (*The sound of the motor boat.*) Perfect! The others are here.

(*Duke, Silvia, and Edward enter.*)

Duke: I was just in time. The lake is starting to freeze over.

Juliet: Then your timing was perfection.

(*She goes to Silvia and kisses her on both cheeks, then does the same to Edward.*)

Juliet: (*cont*) My darlings, thank for coming on such a glacial night. Duke, take their coats and put them in the closet. Take Albert's as well.

(*She points to the coat on the chair. Duke collects all the coats and exits.*)

Silvia: What a lovely place! It reminds me of my chalet in the Alps.

Edward: Why, it does indeed. How poetically tasteful. Simple yet warm and welcoming.

Juliet: Indeed. I got the idea for the decor from Silvia's little cabin. You've been there, I take it?

Edward: (*Taking Silvia's hand.*) Last winter. We went up for a skiing holiday.

Juliet: So I heard. I'm so happy for you both.

Silvia: It is pleasing to hear that. I feared you might be feeling a bit of the green eyed monster, jealousy.

Albert: Iago... "O, beware, my lord, of jealousy; It is the green-eyed monster which doth mock. The meat it feeds on; that cuckold lives in bliss."

Silvia: (*Going to Albert.*) And who is this who knows their Shakespeare so well?

Albert: Albert Sherry. At your service.

(*He kisses her hand.*)

Edward: The Albert Sherry?

Albert: The very same.

Edward: It is an honor, sir, to meet you.

(*Albert ignores him and kisses Silvia's hand again.*)

Albert: And it is my honor to meet you, Silvia. I saw you in that awful movie "Sicilian Nights." You were the only beautiful object in it.

Silvia: That movie won the Palme D'or at Cannes.

Albert: The award was for your performance, not for the film. Besides, the director, your former husband, is dead. You are all that survives.

Silvia: I don't know whether to be appalled or appeased.

Juliet: Be both. Albert is a complex soul.

Albert: And a thirsty one. Have you a drink to take off the chill of the evening?

Juliet: Of course. Forgive me, my dears, for my faulty hospitality. Duke?

(*Duke enters.*)

Duke: Yes, Ma'am?

Juliet: Can you fill our guest's glasses for them.

Duke: Yes Ma'am.

(*Duke goes to the table and pours three glasses of of dark, red-brown wine. He hands them to Albert, Silvia, and Edward. He goes to the bench and sits in silence.*)

Edward: (*To Juliet*) Are you having none?

Juliet: (*As she pours herself a goblet of water...*) Not tonight, I think. I'm taking a bit of a cleanse. Besides, when one wants purity, one drinks water. A toast! To health, love, and money. May we all have time to enjoy them.

(*They clink their glasses together and drink.*)

Albert: What is this swill?

Edward: (*He swirls the wine in his glass, sniffs it, and smiles.*) I believe it is a fine Amontillado from Jerez, with a touch of Cointreau and the barest hint of peaches. Something else I can't quite identify.

Juliet: Why Edward, I had no idea you were a sommelier.

Silvia: All young poets are required to be experts in wine.

Albert: A bit too thick for my taste. (*To Juliet.*) Do you have anything else?

Juliet: I fear not. I thought this would be perfect for tonight's salon.

Albert: Then it will have to do. (*He downs the wine.*) I'll have another.

(*Duke rises, refills his glass, and sits again.*)

Silvia: Juliet, what have you got planned?

Juliet: A very special event. I have been studying Tarot reading with a young mystic in the village. Though I'm not half the poet that Edward is, I did readings for each of you and wrote some verses based on the meaning revealed by the cards. I thought I would share my poems with you and we could discuss them, and perhaps even improve them. An evening to explore creation, destruction, new beginnings. What do you say?

Edward: What fun.

Albert: I doubt it. When did you become a poet, Juliet?

Juliet: I have always been a poet. It is just now I have chosen to reveal my gift. I chose you three to be here because of the special place each of you holds in my life.

Silvia: A splendid idea. I need a bit of culture in my life to remind me that all existence is not about fleeing the paparazzi.

Juliet: Then let us begin. Can we refill any glasses first?

(*All hold out their goblets. Duke refills them.*)

Juliet: (*cont*) Since we have a superb Shakespearean among us, I'd like you, Albert, to begin. Here is the poem I wrote for you.

(*She hands him the poem. He looks it over with a frown.*)

Albert: This is a poem? Where are the stanzas? The rhymes?

Juliet: It's modern, you know. Free verse. Isn't that the way it's done these days, Edward.

Edward: Most certainly. Rhyme and static form died years ago.

Albert: Balderdash!

Juliet: Just read it and then we will talk about the quality.

Albert: If you insist. A Reading for Albert:

"1. Animal
A clubfoot lion
Waits red
At the end of the hedge
There will be no error
Walk stone by stone onto
The path
It is well for him to maintain
It is a door
Or a window
There will be good fortune

2. Mineral
Lapis and topaz
Sift between
Tomorrow and his hands
He will suffer the small
There will be evil

3. Vegetable
The spring brings rain
And thinner hair
And fat carrots
There will be no mistake
I have laid my seed
One to a space

54

And see the green
There will be progress and success
It seems fine
This year
There is peril

4. Air
The birds have left
White bones
For the wind to polish
There is no occasion for sadness
It could have been
A door
Or a window
There will be cause for regret
Look at the table
Empty glasses

His companions will come
And share in his happiness"

Silvia: Splendid, and so well presented.

Edward: So impressionist. Juliet, you have indeed become a poet.

Albert: Posh and twaddle! I have no idea what this means. What has happened to clarity and meaning?

Juliet: What could be more clear? The clubfoot lion is you, dear.

Albert: Me? Are you mad?

Juliet: It's just a metaphor. Are you not a lion on the stage?

Albert: Of course I am, but I'll be damned if I let you call me deformed.

(*He downs his wine and holds out the goblet to Duke, who rises and fills it.*)

Edward: Listen to the words. There will be no error. There will be good fortune. There will be no mistake.

Albert: (*Looking at the poem.*) He will suffer the small. There will be evil. There is peril. Is this what you think of me?

Juliet: I think you are a wonderful actor. Not much more, unfortunately.

Albert: Damn you, woman!

Silvia: Be calm, be calm. Remember the ending. His companions will come and share in his happiness.

Albert: So this is what poetry has come to. (*He drains the glass. Duke refills it. Alberts sits in one of the chairs and pouts.*)

Juliet: Well, I for one thought the reading was marvelous. Silvia, would you like to go next?

(*She hands the poem to Silvia.*)

Silvia: A Reading for Silvia:

"1. A bound woman
Swords around her
You will be cursed
For the works of your hand
The good will be ashes
To them
Oh the blind
Are in control

2. The poet observes
The sea, the world
In one hand, a staff
In the other
She has been with the sea
Smaller than foam lost
In greater than

3. He rides a slow horse
And ignores all symbols
A young foreigner
Will arrive in you
He will see
Through you
He will be free

4. He sits in judgment
The sword of life
And death
Dark haired men walk slowly
To you, the seal of the crown
Is ripped from your hands
The bitterness
In them
In you

5. A blind woman
Balances two swords
A moon
Oh this cannot be good
The two are one
This has been
And they
Are falling
Back to the earth

6. A merchant gives
Money to the poor
Now is the proper time
Beware
Be of good cheer
Beware
You will be gratified
Beware

7. The world a wreath
A veil
The time for a voyage
She said I will travel
And be the ends of the Universe
I will control
That which is lost

8. A young man
Before the chalices
The vision
Nothing true is suggested
Love the false for that
Is God's face

9. Calmly he watches
The ships at sea
One bears his own image
One day it will come
One is home from a new
World, can this be it
And is Slowly coming
Into view, is it time

10. Two are chained
To the devil
A storm races the
Children home"

Edward: Stunning! I believe she's captured you.

Albert: Posh and twaddle.

Edward: No, no. Don't you see? A talented woman, lost in her fame, seeking love and redemption. A young hero comes to free her. They travel to the ends of the universe. Silvia, it is you and me.

Silvia: Yes, there is that. But what about "now is the proper time. Beware. Be of good cheer. Beware. You will be gratified. Beware?" Where did that come from?

Juliet: You remember the first time we met?

Silvia: In Milan, at the opera.

Juliet: Edward, Silvia was the most beautiful woman I ever saw. I had to find out what it would be like to be with such a specimen. There was a party after the show. We both got a bit smashed and ended up in bed together. I had never been with a woman before...I'm not so sure about Silvia, she seemed so self-assured. After that, we met many times but never discussed that night. For me it was very special. How about for you, Silvia.

Silvia: How dare you talk about this in front of company!

(*She finishes her glass and Duke refills it. She chugs it down. He refills it again.*)

Juliet: Sometimes truth will out. Isn't that so, Edward?

Edward: (*He takes Silvia's hand. She swats it away.*) Is it true? Is it...look, it doesn't matter. We have all experimented. It is just you and me and the future. The past is a distant dream.

Silvia: (*To Juliet.*) How can you be so cruel?

(*Silvia goes to the chair next to Albert and sits, angry and sullen.*)

Juliet: Honesty is not cruelty. All the poets know that. You see, even Edward forgives you.

(*She hands Edward his poem.*)

Juliet: (*cont*) Perhaps his poem will make you feel better. Can you read for us, Edward?

Edward: I shall do my best. A reading for Edward:

"1. Earth
A blue flower, a cow eats it
A river, dark and on fire
A tree is hiding all the secrets
Hand me an ax, brother

2. Water
A river, dark and on fire
Sunrise waits in the air

Behind the mountains
The darkness reminds itself
Of the last time
The sun rose on the river

3. Fire
This is what can be, ashes
This is what can be done

4. Air
Sunrise waits in the air
Behind the mountains
The sky is a serpent's eye
All we can see of it
The darkness reminds itself
Of the last time
Prepares itself

5. Blue
A blue flower, a cow eats it
You have been rosy-eyed
In the face of morning
It and me and the space between
Hand me an ax, brother

6. Yellow
The sky is a shepherd's eye
All we can see of it
You will have success
On some normal path

A tree is hiding all the secrets
Prepares itself

7. Red
You have been crimson-eyed
In the face of morning
Dew is falling on all sides
It and me and the space between
Sunrise on the river

8. White
You will have success on some normal path
Something is moving, there, among the hills
This is what can be, an ash
There at your right hand

9. Space
Dew is falling on all sides
This is what can be of the end times
Sunrise on the river

10. Light
Something is moving
There, at your right hand
Hand me an ax
And the space between
Sunrise waits on the river
A cow eats it
A blue flower
Is hiding all the secrets"

Juliet: Amazing, if I say so myself.

Edward: Hand me an ax, brother? Do you think of me as destructive?

Juliet: Oh, that's just a small part of it. "The darkness reminds itself of the last time" is the line that reminds most of our little tryst.

Albert: (*Slurring*) Ha! There's the rub!

(*Silvia leaps up, a bit unsteady.*)

Silvia: Edward! You and Juliet?

Edward: It was long before I met you. I couldn't resist the temptation of an older woman. After all, you and I are a bit the same.

Silvia: (*Draining her glass. Duke refills it.*) I will never be like her. She is a scorpion, an anaconda squeezing the life out of all she touches!

Juliet: More like a praying mantis, my dear. At least I don't eat my victims.

Edward: (*Draining his glass. Duke refills it.*) I never realized how cruel you could be.

Juliet: Life is all about learning. Sit down, Edward. I have a poem about myself.

(*Edward sits next to Albert and Silvia. He tries to take her hand. She swats it away. Juliet picks up her poem.*)

Juliet: A reading for Juliet:

"1. I don't know
Let's think it over, visions, the past
The journey

2. Doubt destroys faith
A small white dog at your heels
And a sun and the mountains
And the blue cool air
That you step into
These will be your problems

3. An unusual courtship
Two ships in the background juggle the sea
The man in control is standing on his head
Infinity
This is the best you can hope for

4. Thoughts are things
Isis unveiled must only sit
In a long white cloth
And wait for the forest to gather
This is the basis of the matter

5. The truth
A rider approaches the river, puts the cup
To his lips and sips slowly
This is his past

6. Emotion and intellect
There is a lady in a yellow robe
With three cats, a staff
In one hand, sunflower in the other
A choice
This will come

7. The struggle to maintain balance
She is surrounded by swords
Her eyes are bound
The water laps at her feet
A small house behind her, on a cliff
Of sand and mud

8. Sacrifice or expiation
The hanged man
New leaves at his branches
This will be around you

9. A short journey
There is a hand coming from the clouds
A hedgerow, flowers, a gate
This is what you hope for
This is what you fear

10. The sun
No one can hurt you
There has been a child
A wall, a white horse
A garden, a home
But just for now
A circle of love protects you
This will be"

Albert: A circle of love. I'd say more the web of a black widow. This night has sickened me.

(*He staggers out the door. We hear him vomiting.*)

(*Silvia rises unsteadily.*)

Silvia: And to think I once thought of you as a friend.

(*She staggers out the door. We hear her vomiting.*)

Edward: (*Rising unsteadily*) The hanged man. I should have known.

(*He staggers out the door. We hear him vomiting.*)

Juliet: Oh dear. I had hoped for a better response. I guess you are my only audience, Duke. What did you think of the poems?

Duke: I don't know much about poetry, Ma'am. I do know a few limericks...there was an old man from Nantucket...

Juliet: Yes, I know that one, dear. No need to recite the whole thing. Can you go check on our guests?

(*Duke goes out the door, then rushes back in.*)

Duke: Ma'am! Ma'am! Oh my God! They're all dead!

Juliet: Oh dear. What a tragedy.

Duke: What should we do? The lake is frozen and I can't get back to town.

Juliet: Perhaps...wait...I know. Put them in the snowbank. We don't want them stinking up the yard.

Duke: In the snowbank?

Juliet: Yes. And throw a few shovelfuls of snow on top.

(*She finishes her glass of water.*)

Juliet: (*cont*) Ah, the purity of water. Duke, I'm going to prepare for bed. Will you join me after you take care of ... them?

Duke: Yes Ma'am. Whatever you say.

(Juliet blows him a kiss and exits. Duke watches her go, shakes his head. He goes to the serving table and pours himself a glass of wine. He downs it, looks at the door where Juliet left, pours another and downs it. He goes out the other door.)

Darkness.

The end

WALKING THE DOG
a radio play

SPOKEN WITH LITTLE EMOTION, AS IN THE
PROLOGUE OF A GREEK TRAGEDY.

He: I was walking the dog.

She: I was walking the dog.

Both: We were walking the dog.

He: The sun was out.

She: The sun was out and the mountains seemed to glow.

He: They glowed in the light of the rising sun.

She: The snow was gone and mud season was over.

Both: We were walking the dog. She was slow and full of pain.

He: But still she enjoyed the crisp air.

She: She was arthritic and had scabs on her head and paws.

He: She was wobbly and old.

She: Her muzzle was grey.

He: Her tail was going bald.

She: Her tail once was curled into a scimitar...

He: And she held it high above her haunches...

She: And she wagged it and walked...

He: With springs in her knees...

She: With a swagger and a grin.

Both: We were walking (*pause*) the dog.

He: I was (*pause*) walking the dog...

She: I was (*pause*) walking the dog...

He: And she had an open sore...

She: An open sore on her head...

He: A bleeding wound on her head...

She: And still she sniffed at everything.

He: At everything, the invasive yellow iris...

She: At everything, the excrement of other dogs...

He: At everything, the posts and trees and wild roses...
Both: That other dogs had pissed on.
She: Her nose was like the eyes of the morning.
He: She was reading the morning paper.
She: She was checking out the neighborhood news.
Both: We were walking the dog.
He: She barked at a squirrel in the road.
She: She was still so interested in life.
He: She was off the leash and wandering...
She: Along the side of the road.
He: She looked up at us...
She: With just a trace of puppy...
He: With just a trace of what had once been.
Both: We heard the growl streaking down the hill...
She: From the hill where the barking pit bull lived...
He: From the house where the wheel-less rusting truck lived.
Both: We saw the pit bull at the same time...
She: But there wasn't enough time...
He: There wasn't enough time to react.
She: The pit bull leapt across the shoulder of the road...
He: And onto our dog...
She: Our aged happy dog...
He: And buried his teeth into her neck.
She: I could only scream no no no.
He: I ran to the mass of writhing dogs.
She: He ran to the dogs, he grabbed a stick.
He: I beat the pit bull, I kicked him in the ribs...
She: And then the animal dropped his grip...
He: And stared at me with hate in his yellow eyes...

She: With hateful yellow eyes, and crouched as if about to leap...

He: And crouched and paused and ran back up the hill...

Both: As its owners came rushing down at us.

She: The man staggered as he ran.

He: The man had red eyes and a beer belly.

She: The man swung his booted leg.

He: The boot caught the pit bull under the chin.

She: It flew into the bushes and shook its head and ran...

He: It ran back to its own yard.

She: The woman had black eyes that had not slept.

He: The woman had black eyes from a recent beating.

Both: Our dog was lying on the ground.

(*pause*)

Both: Our dog was moving but could not get up.

She: There was blood on her neck.

He: I was shaking with anger and adrenaline.

She: I was shaking and wailed "your dog did this."

He: The woman put her hands on her hips.

She: The woman said our dog should have been on a leash...

He: And walked back to her trashy house on the hill.

She: If I had a gun...

He: I picked our baby up.

She: He picked her up and carried her home.

He: There was blood on my shirt.

She: You started the car. I called the vet.

He: She is buried in the shade of the front yard spruce.

She: It was her favorite place.

He: If her spirit could climb to the top of the tree...
She: She could see the top of Whiteface Mountain.
Both: And fly away.

PASSION VINE

Cast of Characters

Ed - A middle-aged man in city clothes: shirt with collar, khaki slacks, baseball cap. The cuffs of his pants are muddy and there are sweat stains under his arms. He has a week old beard and his hair is unkempt. He has a posh "laptop plus" backpack.

Stan - A middle-aged mountain man with flannel shirt, stained blue jeans, ragged boots, long hair and full beard.

Angie - Stan's ex-wife. She is wearing a designer blouse and tight, skinny jeans.

Setting

Interior. A small cabin in the High Peaks. Early Fall. There is a fireplace with a pile of wood stacked against the wall, a kitchen with a wood-burning stove, a sink with a hand-operated pump for water, a table with four wooden chairs, and a single bed. In one corner is a rocking chair. On one wall are open shelves with clothes, sleeping bags, a few random household goods. A kerosene lantern and box of matches sit on a sideboard next to a few plates and cups and a tray with silverware. Pots and pans hang near the stove and a coffee percolator sits at the ready. A window over the sink reveals a panorama of mountains when the sun is out and moonlight when it is not.

(*Early afternoon. There is a banging at the door.*)

Ed: (*offstage*) Stan! Hello? Anybody home?

(*The door opens. Ed enters slowly, looking around for Stan. He does not close the door.*)

Ed: Stan? Anybody home?

(*Ed takes off his backpack and tosses it to the floor by the bed. He goes to the table and sits, hanging his head. He starts to shudder violently, crosses his arms on his chest and squeezes. The shaking stops. He goes to the bed and collapses. A head appears in the doorway. It is Stan. He looks around and enters stealthily. He has a rifle in one hand, and a dead rabbit in the other. He sees the man on the bed, drops the rabbit, and points the gun at Ed.*)

Stan: On your feet, asshole!

Ed: (*sits up startled, shivers, rubs his eyes*) Stan...is that you?

Stan: Who the hell? Damn! Ed?

Ed: Yeah.

Stan: You look like shit. (*He puts the gun in the corner and gives Ed a hug.*)

Ed: Feel like it, too. (*He has another shiver-fit.*)

Stan: So what's up? You get city sick or something? Haven't seen you since what...8 to 10 years? You looked a whole lot better then.

Ed: I missed you too. Hiking up here took it out of me. (*Pause*) Sit down, Stan. I've got a problem and need your help.

(*They both sit down at the table. Ed has another shiver-fit.*)

Ed: Here's the deal. I don't know how to say it nice, so here it is straight. I'm a god damned heroin addict, Stan. I came here to dry out.

Stan: Come again?

Ed: You've got to help me, Stan. I've got nowhere else to go.

Stan: How about one of those fancy rehab places? You've got the money.

Ed: Nobody can know! I'll lose my entire clientele if this gets out.

Stan: But why me? Why here? I don't know diddly about addiction. I don't even drink or smoke since I moved to the woods.

Ed: Don't you see? It's perfect! You're so off-grid no one will ever know.

Stan: What if you get all sick and die on me? Angie, you remember my ex, Angie? She's a social worker now and says you need medical monitoring when you go through withdrawal, and you've got the shakes pretty bad.

Ed: Angie...you still see Angie? She was pretty upset when you decided to ditch civilization and become a hermit.

Stan: She forgave me. Figured out I just wasn't happy with life in what she calls the real world. I was making her miserable anyway. I think she was happy to be rid of me.

Ed: Do you ever see her?

Stan: Yeah, we're probably better friends now than when we were married. She comes up every few weeks to bring me stuff she thinks I need, like toothpaste and toilet paper. I just thank her and give her a hug and throw it all away when she leaves.

Ed: You don't brush your teeth or wipe your butt?

Stan: Make my own soap. Works fine. Grow my own corn. Those cobs have more than one use. I do go into town occasionally and sell vegetables at the Farmer's Market, then use the money for things I need that I can't grow or shoot.

(*Ed starts to shiver and sits shakily on the bed.*)

Ed: You've got the life, man. I am so sick of big town hustle. Can you let me stay?

Stan: I don't know. I'm pretty much a loner and I don't think there's much I can do for you if you go all sick on me?

Ed: It's been a couple of days since I shot up. Hopefully, the worst will be over in a day or two more. How about it, Stan? Can I stay? I'll sleep on the floor and keep out of your way.

Stan: Man, this is such a ...How'd you get like this?

Ed: Lost my way. Had a beautiful wife, but she wanted kids and was always on me to do more and be better. I just wanted to have fun. Guess I wasn't much of a catch. Got a few girlfriends along the way and she found out and that was that. The night she left I went out to a bar to drink away the memories and picked up a young hottie. She was a stunner, I tell you, a real hellcat in bed. Threw my back out that night trying to keep up with her. Started on some oxycontin. Man, that was a trip. No more pain. My doctor finally cut me off...said I was becoming dependent. He was sure right.

One of my clients was a dealer. He hooked me up with some heroin. End of story. Here I am.

(*Angie comes in the door. She is wearing city jeans and blouse, but is carrying designer shoes in her hands and wearing hiking boots. She has a well-used backpack.*)

Angie: Surprise! (*She rushes across the room and embraces Stan.*)

Stan: Angie! What a fine surprise! I didn't expect to see you for another week or two.

Angie: You are so cut off up here. The city council couldn't pass their budget, so all the public employees got put on unpaid leave. I have at least a few days off, or maybe more if those putzes in city hall don't get their act together. I figured you'd be out of some basics by now, so I brought you a few necessities.

(*She opens her backpack and starts unloading her gifts on the table. There are several books, a handful of candles, a couple of boxes of matches, and a pair of dress shoes.*)

Stan: Thanks. (*He picks up the items one by one.*)
Good, useful. (*He picks up the shoes.*) What the hell are these for?

Angie: Just in case you ever want to come into town and look like a civilized person.

Stan: Not likely.

(*Angie notices Ed.*)

Angie: You have company.

Stan: Indeed I do. Angie, you remember Ed, my old college roommate? Ran off to the city and became a big-time lawyer.

Angie: Ed! Of course I remember! Damn, you look terrible. (*Backing off and looking Ed over.*) Are you sick?

(*Ed is silent, looks at his feet.*)

Stan: Tell her.

Ed: I, uh, I...

Stan: Tell her. She works with people like you.

(*Angie tosses Stan a quizzical glance, then looks back at Ed.*)

Ed: I, uh, I...I'm addicted to heroin. I came here to go through withdrawal. (*He shivers.*)

Angie: (*suddenly business-like*): Let me see your arms.

(*She takes his hand, pushes back his sleeve, and examines his arm.*)

Angie: (*cont*) Collapsed veins. How long since your last shot?

Ed: (*Glancing at Stan*) Two days.

Angie: We can't help if you can't be honest.

Ed: OK. This morning.

(*She turns to Ed and trips over the rabbit.*)

Angie: What the...Oh, good. (*To Stan.*) Take this out and skin it. He'll need some protein. You have a fire in the stove?

Stan: (*As he walks out the door with the rabbit.*) Should be some embers.

(*Angie grabs a couple of small logs and puts them in the stove, fills a pot with water and puts it directly on top of the firebox, then turns to Ed.*)

Angie: Did you bring any heroin with you?

Ed: No.

Angie: How about any other drugs?

Ed: No.

Angie: How about alcohol?

Ed: (*looking at his feet*) No.

Angie: Right. Where is it?

Ed: In the backpack.

(*Angie goes to the backpack and pulls out a bottle of vodka.*)

Ed: (*cont*) I thought it would take the edge off.

Angie: Look. You're not going to sleep tonight, and maybe not tomorrow night. You're going straight to hell, my friend, and this bottle will look like your best buddy. When the suffering gets bad you'll drink it all in about an hour and die of alcohol poisoning before midnight. (*She goes to the sink and pours out the vodka.*) Now get your clothes off and get in bed.

Ed: That's Stan's. I can lay on the floor.

Angie: Don't make me hit you. Get in the damn bed.

(*Ed reluctantly goes over to the bed and begins undressing. He turns his back to Angie, strips, and gets under the covers, shivering.*)

(*Stan returns with a pan of rabbit parts. He puts them on the counter by the sink.*)

Stan: What's the verdict?

Angie: He's in for a god-awful night. Sweats, aches and pains all over, no sleep, and probably diarrhea. Is the outhouse clean?

Stan: Well, you know I've been up here alone for several months. It's not...

Angie: OK. I'll go clean it up.

(*She fills a pail with water, grabs a rag from a drawer in the sideboard, and leaves.*)

Ed: She's quite a woman.

Stan: (*Looks over at the bed and sees Ed.*) Better now than when she was with me.

Ed: I beg your pardon?

Stan: Just a joke. She's my ex, but we're pretty open about, well, life in general. She had at least one other boyfriend in college and I know he wanted to marry her. Why she chose me I'll never know. Said she needed a real man.

Ed: (*Long pause.*) I always wondered why you gave up your Dad's business and pulled this Adirondack hermit thing.

Stan: I couldn't seem to catch on with any job. Kept getting fired for going on a hike and not showing up for work. I just couldn't see the point of dedicating my life to making money. Folks said it was like I was incompetent or something. But I just didn't care.

Ed: What happened with Angie?

Stan: She moved up here with me at first, but couldn't take the isolation. She's one of those people who need people around her to be happy. Guess I just didn't get it. Left a note on the table saying she couldn't do it anymore. All for the best, really. We're both happier now.

Ed: She ever hook up with someone else?

Stan: Naw. Claims she's happy on her own. Guess we're more alike than either one of us cares to admit.

(*Angie returns with the bucket and rag and an armful of vines with golf ball sized fruit on them.*)

Angie: Ed, you are one lucky smack freak. Look what I found growing on the outhouse! (*She puts the vines on the table.*) Passion Vine!

Stan: That weed? Makes a pretty flower, for sure. Just sort of came up one year.

Angie: I'm surprised it grew this far north. Usually doesn't do well in the colder climates. But it sometimes does, and thanks be. I've got one growing in my apartment. Beautiful flowers and tasty fruit. Ed, this is going to save your cookies!

Ed: (*Shivers.*) How so?

Angie: Tea from the leaves will keep you hydrated and help with the body aches. Minerals in the fruit help with some of the withdrawal symptoms. If we had internet up here, you could check it out online. It's an all around cure and an aphrodisiac to boot. Life is sweet!

Stan: How do you know this stuff?

Angie: You taught me to rely on nature when I got sick. Not sure if you were trying to avoid going to the pharmacy in Lake Placid when I was ill or if you had gone totally herbal. But I learned then, and have learned even more now. My friends in town call me Mother Earth!

(*She grabs a cup and fills it with hot water from the stove, immerses some Passion Vine leaves in the cup, and washes off some of the fruit. She offers the fruit to Ed.*)

Angie: (*cont*) Eat up, addict.

Ed: (*Chewing one.*) Damn. These are pretty sour.

Angie: Not quite ripe. Eat them anyway.

(*Ed downs the rest of them.*)

Angie: (*cont*) Now wash them down with this. (*She hands him a cup of the tea. He drinks it.*)

Ed: Not too bad.

Angie: Now just lay back down and pray you don't shit Ed's bed.

(*Ed pulls the covers over his head. We see him shiver.*)

Stan: Damn odd seeing him like this after all these years.

Ed: I can hear you!

Stan: Good. You hungry?

Ed: Been three days since I ate.

Angie: I'll cook up some rabbit stew.

(*She starts to prepare dinner. Stan pulls up a chair next to Ed.*)

Stan: So, old buddy, how'd it come to this?

Ed: Don't blame me, blame the doctor. The bastard turned me into an addict!

Stan: Did you try to stop?

Ed: I tried, but the pain kept coming back. The damned doctor cut me off. Said I didn't need it anymore, but man, he was dead wrong. The pain wouldn't go away. I tried physical therapy, yoga, mindful meditation, but nothing helped. Fucking doctors...it's all their fault!

Stan: You had nothing to do with it?

Ed: Whose side are you on, anyway? None of this would have happened it they hadn't put me on opioids!

Stan: What the hell kind of excuse it that? Aren't you responsible for your own actions?

Ed: Fuck you, Stan!

Angie: (*setting the table with three bowls of stew*) Men! All you do is blame, blame, blame! Cut the crap and come and eat! Now! That's an order!

(*Stan and Ed stare darts at each other. Stan comes to the table and sits. Ed wraps the blanket around Stan's shoulder and joins him. The three eat in silence for a bit; Stan and Ed stare at their plates. Angie looks back and forth at the two of them.*)

Angie: So, children...are you quite finished?

(*They both nod.*)

Angie: (*cont*) Take the dishes to the sink. Stan, you wash. Ed, you dry. Try to act like adults.

(*She pulls a book out of her backpack, sits in the rocking chair, and starts to read.*)

(*Ed and Stan begin to do the dishes. When they are almost done, Ed, still with the shakes, drops a dish on the floor and it shatters. Stan says nothing, grabs a broom and sweeps up the mess. He goes to the door.*)

Stan: I'm going to sleep outside tonight. Need some peace and quiet.

(*He grabs a sleeping bag and slams the door as he leaves. Angie gets up and pours some hot water over a handful of passion vine leaves. She stirs it for a few moments and hands the cup to Ed.*)

Angie: I need some peace and quiet too. Drink this, get in that bed, and try to calm down.

(*Ed drinks down the brew, gets in the bed, and huddles under the covers. We can hear an occasional moan and see him shaking. Angie reads and tries to ignore him, but the moaning gets louder. She goes over to sit on the edge of the beds and strokes his forehead.*)

Ed: Cold, so cold. (*Shivers*)

Angie: Hang in there, Ed. It's just a part of the process.

Ed: Freezing...is there another blanket?

(*Angie looks around, can't find one.*)

Angie: Sorry. It will all go away in a few hours.

(*Angie continues to stroke Ed's head.*)

Ed: (*He sits up and takes her hand.*) Thanks for your help, Angie. I'm really sorry it didn't work out between you and Ed. (*Pause.*) Does he know about us?

Angie: Look, Ed. You and I were just a brief interlude. He never found out and I never told him. You were, I guess, a way of testing my love for Stan. He won.

Ed: But we were pretty good together, weren't we?

Angie: Good in bed, but not much else, I'm afraid. It always felt like you were just trying to put one over on poor Stan. Prove you were more of a man than he was. Like you were jealous of him.

Ed: But I cared for you.

Angie: It felt like you cared for yourself.

Ed: I asked you to marry me.

Angie: And I said no. Look at you now. Guess I made the right decision.

Ed: You chose Stan instead, then left him. How is that the right decision?

Angie: At least he knew who he was. I respected him then, and still do. We weren't so good together, but we became best friends after the split. I can share almost everything with him, even now.

Ed: Almost?

Angie: Almost. I actually came here today to tell him...

(*Stan enters. He sees Angie and Ed holding hands on the bed.*)

Stan: What the hell?

(*Angie stands up awkwardly and walks over to Stan.*)

Angie: Look, we were just...(*She tries to take his hands in hers, but he pushes her away.*)

Stan: Just sitting on the bed playing kissy face is my guess. You two decide to get together again? Need this junky to complete your life?

Angie: Again? You knew?

Stan: Of course, I knew. Everybody knew.

Angie: But you never said...

Stan: What would be the point? Sometimes you just have to accept the things you cannot change. I got lucky...you figured him out before making a huge mistake.

Ed: Figured me out? What kind of shit is that? I loved this girl!

Stan: You loved sticking it to me. You never could handle me being more of a man than you.

Ed: (*Gets in Stan's face.*) You were just a man who couldn't keep his girl! Couldn't even keep her after you got her!

Angie: (*Getting between the two men.*) Stop it! This isn't about you! It's...it's about me.

(*Both men step back and stare at Angie.*)

Angie: (*cont*) Stan, I loved you dearly, but you were the first man in my life. I didn't want to make a mistake. Ed, I apologize...I took up with you to test my feelings for Stan. I needed to see if my feelings for him were true or not. You were...an experiment. I'm sorry.

Ed: An experiment? My god, just an experiment?

Angie: And a successful one. I found out that Stan was the one for me.

Stan: Then why did you leave?

Angie: I couldn't live the way you needed to live. Out here in the woods, all alone? I suppose I needed more than just you. And you clearly needed this more than you needed me. Am I wrong? Aren't you happier now than you were with me in the house?

Stan: Look, Angie...I'm sorry I failed you.

Angie: You didn't fail. You are who you are, and I love that. I just couldn't live with it. (*Pause.*) I came here today to tell you something. You know Clarence Blister?

Stan: The accountant? Wife died in a car accident or something.

Angie: That's the one. Left him with two small daughters. I...started seeing him a few months ago. He asked me to marry him. I said yes.

Ed and Stan (*together*): You're going to marry an accountant?

Angie: Yes, I am. We care for each other and I love the kids. It's kind of what I always wanted...a family and children and stability. Something I couldn't find with either of you.

Stan: But...an accountant?

Angie: Not everyone can be a mountain man. Not everybody needs one.

(*Ed begins to cough uncontrollably. He sits back down on the bed.*)

Stan: Talk about not a mountain man. (*Angie goes to Ed and sits him down in the rocking chair.*)

Angie: Two icons of manhood. Ed, when do you have to go back to the city?

Ed: I took a month off.

Angie: Good. You'll need at least that long to start feeling normal. Stan, you know that rehab place down in Saranac Lake?

Stan: I think so.

Angie: Get him down there tomorrow. See what help they can be. Now I need some sleep. You have another sleeping bag?

Stan: Yeah.

Angie: Good. You two can camp out on the porch and pretend you're back in college, camping out and sleeping under the stars. Ed won't be able to sleep anyway. You can talk all night. I'm taking the bed.

(*She gets into the bed and pulls the covers over her head. Stan turns out the lights. The room is dimly lit by the moon.*)

(*Ed pulls on his clothes and approaches Stan.*)

Ed: I'm sorry, man. I kind of lost my head.

Stan: Got it. Me too. (*pause*) She's right, you know.

Ed: Right?

Stan: I kind of dropped out of life.

Ed: Me too.

Stan: Couple of places in Lake Placid that bring in bands on the weekend. Want to go after you get out of rehab?

Ed: Haven't actually danced in years. Think anyone would want to hang out with a couple of old middle aged geezers like us?

Stan: Only one way to know. (*He picks up the city shoes on the table.*) I might even find a use for these.

Ed: You're on.

Stan: I'm too hyped to lay down. I'm going to the outhouse and harvest some more of that Passion Vine. Two old geezers just may need some extra help.

(*They slap each other on the shoulder and exit. Angie sits up in bed and shakes her head, goes to the sink and begins to wash the remaining dishes, her back to the audience. She begins to shiver, and it appears she may be crying. She turns around, hugs herself, and smiles. She breaks into laughter.*)

Darkness.

The end.

Early in his career, Charles had an underground play ("Visigoths") produced in Los Angeles, which led to script writing contracts for several TV series, including "Kojack" and "Here Come the Brides." He fled Hollywood, got an MFA in poetry, and went to Iran to teach literature at several Universities. For five years, he edited Seizure, a magazine of poetry and fiction, which received a grant from the National Foundation for the Arts/Coordinating Council of Literary Magazines. He has also been a cab driver, social worker on Skid Row in Los Angeles, refugee worker in camps in Malaysia, Indonesia, and Costa Rica, and owner of a tour company. Recent work includes stories, essays, and poems published in Liebamour, Writers Bloc, Commonline Journal, The Bactrian Room, Scythe, L'Amour Fou, Adirondack Life, and Blueline. His poems and stories have been anthologized in "Road Poets," "Adirondack Epiphanies," "Schroon River Anthology," and "Karma in the High Peaks," which won the "People's Choice Award" for best book of 2010 from the Adirondack Center for Writing. His poems won the Patricia and Emmett Robinson Prize (2015) and first place at the North Country Writers Festival twice. His most recent books are a collection of short stories, "Raptures" and a collection of poems, "Waking Up in a Beautiful Room." He currently splits his time between Lake Placid, NY, and Charleston, SC.

charles@envisionist.com